BUILD BACK BETTER SECTOR GUIDES
VOLUME 4: IRRIGATED AGRICULTURE

OCTOBER 2024

ASIAN DEVELOPMENT BANK

CONTENTS

TABLES AND BOXES

ACKNOWLEDGMENTS

Preparation of this *Build Back Better Sector Guides* series was led by Belinda Hewitt, senior disaster risk management specialist, Climate Change and Sustainable Development Department (CCSD), ADB with substantive inputs and review from Brigitte Balthasar, senior disaster and climate risk financing specialist, CCSD, ADB; Charlotte Benson, former principal disaster risk management Specialist, ADB; Alexandra Galperin, unit head, disaster risk management, CCSD, ADB; Steven Goldfinch, senior disaster risk management specialist, CCSD, ADB; Anne Orquiza, senior disaster risk management officer, CCSD, ADB; Grendel Saldevar, senior operations assistant, CCSD, ADB; and Mario Unterwaining, former disaster risk management specialist (resilient infrastructure), ADB. The series was developed in close collaboration with ADB Sectors Group and country teams. Margie Peters-Fawcett copy edited the volumes with the assistance of Cherry Lynn Zafaralla as proofreader. Layout was created by Rommel Marilla, page proofs checking by Levi Rodolfo Lusterio, and administrative support by Michelle Imperial.

This volume was written by Robert Rout with additional drafts, case study inputs, reviews, and contributions to workshops provided by Md. Abul Basher, senior natural resources and agriculture specialist, Sectors Group (SG), ADB; Jelle Beekma and Marie L'Hostis, water resources specialists, SG; Piseth Long, senior project officer, SG; Eric Quincieu, principal water resources specialist, SG; Nathan Rive, senior climate change specialist, CCSD; Geoffrey Wilson, senior water resources specialist, SG; and Asad Zafar, senior project officer (water resources), SG. Peer review by Dana Kanaan is greatly appreciated.

ABBREVIATIONS

ADB	Asian Development Bank
BBB	build back better
DMC	developing member country
DRM	disaster risk management
EAL	Emergency Assistance Loan
EWS	early warning system
NBS	nature-based solutions
PDNA	post-disaster needs assessment
RAP	rapid appraisal process

ADB Indonesia: Emergency Assistance for Rehabilitation and Reconstruction Project (52316-001).
Local communities have benefitted from resilient irrigation systems delivered under the project following the
2018 earthquake and tsunami. The reconstruction of the Gumbasa irrigation network has been completed,
and farmers have returned to the plant paddy.

Typhoon Rammasun (Glenda) passing through Laguna Province, Philippines
with winds in excess of 120 kilometers per hour in the early morning of 16 July 2014.

I

INTRODUCTION

Timely support for recovery and reconstruction efforts is critical when a disaster occurs to minimize any potential long-term setbacks to sustainable and inclusive socioeconomic development. It is essential to provide a window of opportunity to rebuild assets and improve livelihoods to increase climate and disaster resilience and reduce the risk of future hazards. With impacts of disasters projected to rise in the coming decades as affected by climate change, unplanned urbanization, poor risk governance, and a range of other trends, challenges relating to climate uncertainty, growing complexity of infrastructure systems, and the compounding nature of multiple hazard events underline the importance of ensuring that communities and infrastructure systems are equipped to cope, adapt, and recover when faced with future shocks and stresses.

Developing member countries (DMCs) of the Asian Development Bank (ADB) bear a disproportionate share of impacts from geophysical and extreme weather hazard events. Between 2004 and 2023, these DMCs accounted for 55% of global disaster fatalities and 74% of people affected.[1] Over this 20-year period, ADB has provided more than $9.1 billion in financing for emergency assistance loan (EAL) projects relating to disasters triggered by natural hazards, conflict, displacement, food insecurity, and health emergencies. The support that ADB offers its DMCs aims at ensuring resilient post-disaster recovery, as well as strengthening long-term disaster risk reduction.

---

[1] Centre for Research on the Epidemiology of Disasters, EM-DAT: The International Disaster Database. http:// www.emdat.be (accessed 5 February 2024). People affected by multiple disasters have been counted multiple times.

ADB's Strategy 2030[2] and 2021 Disaster and Emergency Assistance Policy[3] outline commitments to ensure effective response and support to build back better (BBB) after a disaster or emergency.[4] Build back better refers to the use of the early recovery and reconstruction phases after a disaster or emergency to increase resilience of nations and communities to future events by integrating risk reduction measures into the restoration of physical infrastructure, societal systems, livelihoods, economies, and the environment.[5] By systematically promoting risk-informed, well-designed, and timely recovery and reconstruction, ADB supports the implementation of international agreements, such as the Sendai Framework for Disaster Risk Reduction 2015–2030 and the 2030 Agenda for Sustainable Development Goals, including its 17 Sustainable Development Goals, both of which promote a comprehensive approach toward disaster risk management (DRM) and BBB frameworks, including through community-based applications.

The six volumes that comprise the *Build Back Better Sector Guides* series aim to support ADB staff, consultants, and DMC counterparts to enhance the climate and disaster resilience of DMC communities, infrastructure, and systems through effective and well-designed post-disaster assistance. The volumes are based on principles, measures, and lessons learned from the international BBB literature; a review of over 40 ADB EALs processed between 2004 and 2021; and the outcome of consultations with a wide range of ADB staff.

Each of the volumes has been co-developed with relevant ADB sector and thematic groups. The sectors are areas in which ADB has played a key role in post-disaster recovery and reconstruction and where majority of ADB's disaster and emergency assistance has focused in the last 20 years. They are as follows:

(i)   Volume 1: Overview
(ii)   Volume 2: Transport
(iii)   Volume 3: Water, Sanitation, and Hygiene (WASH)
(iv)   Volume 4: Irrigated Agriculture
(v)   Volume 5: Social Infrastructure
(vi)   Volume 6: Power

This Volume 4: Irrigated Agriculture provides an overview of good practice solutions, considerations, and lessons learned for building back better in irrigated agriculture systems but does not represent a general or step-by-step handbook on methods to prepare and implement post-disaster needs assessment (PDNA) or EALs; nor does it for other forms of post-disaster assistance.

The scope of this series includes building resilience in response to disasters triggered by natural hazards; however, some of its content is relevant to the broader aspect of economic recovery, including within the context of health emergencies and conflict. Complementary objectives, including equity and inclusion, green recovery, poverty reduction, and broader sustainable development, are also presented.

---

[2]   Asian Development Bank (ADB). 2017. *Strategy 2030: Achieving a Prosperous, Inclusive, Resilient, and Sustainable Asia and the Pacific.*
[3]   ADB. 2021. *Revised Disaster and Emergency Assistance Policy.*
[4]   Strategy 2030 sets out a commitment to "provide assistance for disaster response, including support to build back better."
[5]   Adapted from United Nations General Assembly. 2016. Report of the Open-Ended Intergovernmental Expert Working Group on Indicators and Terminology Relating to DRR. Seventy-First Session, Item 19(c).

ADB's Role in Resilient Post-Disaster Recovery and Reconstruction

Following a disaster, ADB can mobilize rapid post-disaster technical support under the second window of its Asia Pacific Disaster Response Fund in areas such as the preparation of PDNAs; government-led recovery plans; and post-disaster projects, including emergency assistance loans. The post-disaster needs assessment is a well-established tailored methodology that is used for analyzing damage, loss, and needs prioritization. While the exercise should be led by the government, it is often conducted with the support of one or more international partners. The PDNA compiles information relating to the physical impacts of a disaster, economic value of damages and losses, human and macroeconomic impacts, and cost of early and long-term recovery needs and priorities. As such, the PDNA is an important tool to inform implementation of BBB through post-disaster programming.

Once recovery and reconstruction requirements have been assessed, ADB can mobilize finance for recovery and reconstruction through EALs, additional financing for pre-established projects, and investment projects that support longer-term reconstruction needs. ADB's 2021 Emergency Assistance Loan Policy enables the rapid approval of loans (within 12 weeks) to assist in the rebuilding of high-priority physical assets and the restoration of economic, social, and governance activities following disasters triggered by natural hazards, health emergencies, food insecurity, technological and industrial accidents, and post-conflict situations.[6] The Emergency Assistance Loan Policy and Disaster and Emergency Assistance Policy aim to support DMC's BBB efforts to enhance climate and disaster resilience. Table 1 provides a list of additional resources relating to ADB's policies and directives relating to post-disaster assistance.

Table 1: Key Documents on ADB Policies and Guidance for Post-Disaster Assistance

Document	Web Page
2021 Disaster and Emergency Assistance Policy	https://www.adb.org/documents/revised-disaster-and-emergency-assistance-policy
Revised Emergency Assistance Loan Policy	https://www.adb.org/documents/revised-emergency-assistance-loan-policy
Establishment of a Second Window of Assistance under the Asia Pacific Disaster Response Fund	https://www.adb.org/documents/establishment-second-window-assistance-under-asia-pacific-disaster-response-fund
Post-Disaster Needs Assessment Guidelines	https://www.recoveryplatform.org/pdna
Disaster Recovery Planning: Explanatory Note and Case Study	https://www.adb.org/publications/disaster-recovery-planning-explanatory-note-case-study

Source: Asian Development Bank.

---

⁶ ADB. 2021. *Revised Emergency Assistance Loan Policy*.

Importance of Long-Term Resilience Building

Long-term and upstream approaches to resilience building are critical to minimize the impacts of disasters and ensure more effective and efficient use of post-disaster assistance resources. ADB can play a key role in leveraging increased risk awareness to ensure resilience-focused upstream planning. Where risk-responsive socioeconomic development and sector plans are already in place ahead of a disaster, they can more effectively guide long-term disaster recovery and bring about a shift toward resilience and sustainable development.

Risk-informed sector plans enable more rapid and effective post-disaster recovery and reconstruction where they are informed by comprehensive multihazard disaster risk assessments and incorporate ex ante recovery planning. Past ADB EALs, such as the 2015 Nepal: Earthquake Emergency Assistance Project (see Volume 5: Social Infrastructure) and the 2018 Tonga: Cyclone Gita Recovery Project (see Volume 6: Power), aligned recovery planning with climate and disaster resilience objectives set out in existing sector programs, government road maps, and the national development plan.

Use of the Build Back Better Sector Guides

This volume is intended to be read in conjunction with the introductory *Build Back Better Sector Guides—Volume 1: Overview*. The overview guide covers the broad measures that are likely relevant to any post-disaster recovery and reconstruction project, regardless of sector.

While this volume does not provide detailed technical guidance, it does provide various additional technical resources that can guide project-specific decision-making (Appendix: Suggested Readings). For any given project, it is important that resilience measures are selected appropriately and on a project-by-project basis, informed by an understanding of the agricultural system components and local context. There should be analysis of current and future risk; economic development objectives; economic feasibility and viability; as well as relevant policies, including climate and disaster risk management and safeguards requirements.

ADB Bangladesh: Participatory Small-Scale Water Resources Sector Project (39432-013).
ADB is helping Bangladesh establish sustainable small-scale water resources management
systems. The project will develop 230 subprojects in the areas of flood control, drainage,
and irrigation, along with capacity building activities.

ADB Indonesia: Emergency Assistance for Rehabilitation and Reconstruction Project (52316-001).
Local communities have benefitted from resilient irrigation systems delivered under the project following the 2018 earthquake and tsunami. The reconstruction of the Gumbasa irrigation network has been completed, and farmers have returned to the plant paddy.

II

DISASTER IMPACTS AND RECOVERY OBJECTIVES

The agriculture sector is highly impacted by a wide range of natural hazards, causing major economic losses. Asia accounts for 70% of the world's irrigated area;[7] as such, impacts on agricultural infrastructure, particularly in irrigation systems can affect agriculture productivity, livelihoods, and food security. These outcomes are likely to significantly increase over the coming decades, as extreme weather events and long-term changes to precipitation and temperature worsen due to climate change.

The impacts of natural hazards and disasters on agriculture can comprise up to 23% of disaster damage and loss in developing countries.[8] The significant increase in the frequency and intensity of extreme events such as drought, floods, storms, tsunamis, and wildfires observed over the past decades pose a significant challenge to agricultural systems, given their heavy reliance on the natural environment and water resources. This calls for enhanced action to build resilience within the agricultural sector, with post-disaster recovery and reconstruction providing one important window to achieve widescale change.

Emergency assistance from ADB during 2005–2020 in relation to irrigated agriculture represented approximately 7% of total emergency assistance financing and 19% of emergency assistance infrastructure financing.[9] Support included recovery and reconstruction following floods, earthquakes, tsunamis, and tropical storms. Table 2 provides a sample of disaster effects and recovery needs based on five events that occurred during this period.

---

[7]   A. Mukherji and T. Facon. 2009. *Revitalizing Asia's Irrigation to Sustainably Meet Tomorrow's Food Needs*. International Water Management Institute (IWMI) and Food and Agriculture Organization of the United Nations (FAO).

[8]   FAO. 2017. *The Impacts of Disasters on Agriculture: Addressing the Information Gap.*

[9]   Total funding for the period was approximately $7,048 billion, of which $2,523 billion was for infrastructure and $0.362 billion for irrigated agriculture.

Table 2: Agriculture Sector Disaster Effects and Recovery Needs: Examples

Event	Disaster Effects (Damage and Loss) ($ million)		Recovery Needs ($ million)	
	Total	Agriculture	Total	Agriculture
Typhoon Damrey (Viet Nam), 2005	700,000	365,000 (52%)	76,470	6,440 (8%)
Cyclone Sidr and floods (Bangladesh), 2007	3,000,000	1,000,000 (33%)	234,200	64,000 (27%)
Floods (Northern Afghanistan), 2014	240,000	72,000 (30%)	56,660	19,586 (35%)
Earthquake (Palu, Sulawesi Province, Indonesia), 2018	1,700,000	464,739 (27%)	360,000	80,860 (22%)

ADB placed its regular assistance on holder in Afghanistan effective 15 August 2021.
Source: Asian Development Bank.

Following a disaster, priority should be given to restoring agricultural assets and irrigation systems' operations to safeguard livelihoods and food security, restore productivity, and improve resilience to future hazard events. Improvement of infrastructure and irrigation system performance and efficiency should result in systems that are more responsive to hazards, and able to cope with climate change and disasters. Additional objectives for post-disaster recovery are summarized in Box 1.

Box 1: Key Objectives for Post-Disaster Recovery and Reconstruction of Irrigated Agriculture

Global best practices and experience gained by the ADB suggest that in addition to building climate and disaster resilience, the recovery and reconstruction of agricultural assets and irrigation systems should also seek to achieve the following, post-disaster:

- **Enhanced productivity and efficiency of water use** through the adoption of modern and sustainable designs, new technology, and improved methods for system operation and management.
- **Strengthened system management** at the system, institution, and community levels to improve operation and maintenance of assets and systems, productivity, and sustainability.
- **Improved livelihoods and economic development** by improving diversification of income, improved knowledge of communities, increased efficiency of systems and sustainable use of natural resources.

Source: Asian Development Bank.

ADB Pakistan: Trimmu, Panjnad and Islam Barrages Improvement Project (47235-001). Sugarcane is transported to sugar mills. The ADB-supported project rehabilitates and upgrades the Trimmu barrage to irrigate farmlands and to reduce flood risk in Jhang District, Punjab.

ADB Indonesia: Emergency Assistance for Rehabilitation and Reconstruction Project (52316-001). The project delivered resilient irrigation systems near Palu in Central Sulawesi following the 2018 earthquake and tsunami.

III

CLIMATE AND DISASTER RESILIENCE MEASURES

This section provides a description of key measures to enhance the climate and disaster resilience of irrigated agriculture projects in the post-disaster context. The following are based on a review of ADB emergency assistance, staff consultations,[10] and a review of global best practice.

The first step in BBB is to carry out a disaster and climate risk assessment to ensure that infrastructure is rebuilt in a way as to minimize its vulnerability and exposure to future natural hazards. Resilience measures should be confirmed as appropriate on a case-by-case basis and within the context of current and future risks, the local context, economic development objectives and viability, and relevant policies, including safeguards requirements.

Agricultural System Assessment

A post-disaster damage assessment of agricultural systems, including irrigation assets, will provide the basis to classify and prioritize reconstruction and recovery needs, the measures necessary to inform resilience, and improvements required for increased agricultural productivity and efficient usage of land and water resources. A rapid appraisal process (RAP)[11] to categorize system constraints and potential improvements in irrigation infrastructure and management also should take place. The RAP is a knowledge-based toolkit, useful for the speedy and systematic collection, compilation, organization, and analysis of data relating to large canal irrigation systems. The RAP can quantify system performance with parameters (e.g., physical infrastructure, water control, communications, maintenance, institutional capacity, and water delivery service), thus providing a clear picture of problem areas. It enables stakeholders to identify physical constraints and prioritize the steps needed for improvement, the basis for strengthening irrigation system resilience.

---

[10] Consultation workshop on 14 July 2021, with Climate Change and Sustainable Development Department, Central and West Asia Department, South Asia Department, Southeast Asia Department, and East Asia Department.

[11] C. Burt. 2001. Rapid Appraisal Process (RAP) and Benchmarking: Explanation and Tools. Irrigation Training and Research Center. ITRC Report No. R 01-008. California Polytechnic State University.

Resilience includes improvement of existing and new infrastructure to withstand future floods and landslides, as well as more efficient water delivery to reduce percolation loss and, in turn, the impacts of prolonged drought. For example, ADB carried out a RAP of the Bagmati irrigation system in Nepal to identify improvements that were necessary with regard to infrastructure, management, and overall performance.[12] The RAP may also identify resilience opportunities beyond the irrigation system itself—for example, potential for multipurpose irrigation canals to take on the additional function flood conveyance channels in the case of extreme rainfall and flooding.

Assessment tools for RAP should include use of remote sensing imagery for analyses of changes in landform and effects of earthquakes, floods, and drought stress. An example is provided in Box 2.

Box 2: Project Example—Assessment Tools

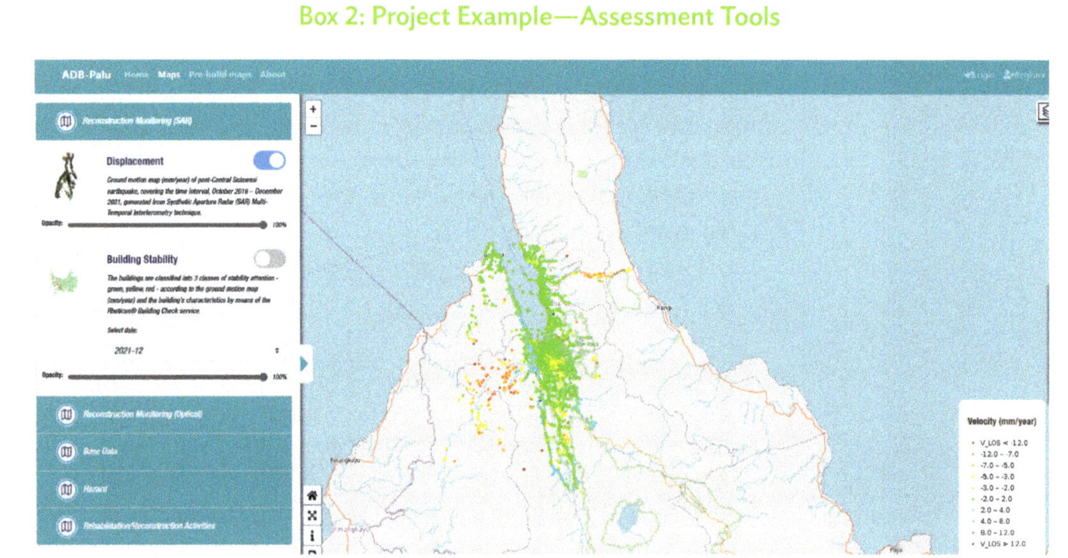

Ground motion map (mm/year) of post-Central Sulawesi earthquake, covering the time interval, October 2018–December 2021. Source: ADB.

Satellite remote sensing is a powerful tool for assessing disaster damages and losses and to support resilient reconstruction. The 2019 **Indonesia: Emergency Assistance for Rehabilitation and Reconstruction Project** (52316-001) leveraged partnerships with the European Space Agency and the Indonesian Space Agency to assess the impacts of a 7.4 magnitude earthquake in Central Sulawesi Province and to monitor the reconstruction and recovery exercise.

A comparison was made of pre- and post-disaster imagery for the mapping of ground deformation and damage to buildings and infrastructure. The results provided the ability to prioritize reconstruction efforts, as well as improve design approaches and construction methods. The monitoring exercise compared reconstruction over two sample areas in two stages (October 2018 and November 2018), for urban and agricultural environments, the latter being related to irrigation channel infrastructure.

Source: ADB. Indonesia: Emergency Assistance for Rehabilitation and Reconstruction Project.

---

[12]   ADB. 2015. *Nepal: Innovations for More Food with Less Water Task 2*. Consultant's Report (45072-001).

Resilient Structures

Post-disaster, repair and/or replacement of essential agriculture infrastructure and restoration of irrigation networks and water services provide an opportunity to improve agricultural system resilience to withstand future events through better design. Design approaches should adopt specifications and standards commensurate with a revised assessment of the frequency and intensity of events (e.g., peak flood flows and return periods), while taking climate change and the potential future scenarios into account, as well as economic development objectives, local context, and economic viability. Climate- and disaster-proofing of infrastructure through resilient site selection, planning, and structural design should be prioritized based on an up-to-date multihazard risk assessment.

For example, to address flood hazard effects on surface irrigation systems, design measures can include an increase in the discharge capacity of emergency spillways to accommodate for more extreme events and in the canal embankment freeboard to cope with higher peak flows. Drainage systems are a complementary component of surface irrigation systems, essential for flood and salinity management, as drainage canals can also be designed to double as irrigation networks during the dry season. In relation to groundwater irrigation systems, well depths may be increased (where environmental impact assessments allow it) to sustain water supply during low recharge periods and ensure resilience to future droughts. In addition, retention ponds to accept rain and storm water during periods of increased precipitation may be introduced.

In areas of high seismic risk, stone masonry structures may be rebuilt with reinforced concrete and the ridged pipelines (steel and/or concrete) of pressure systems may be replaced by high-density polyethylene pipes with flexible joints. Canals may be reconstructed with impermeable Geotech lining and then covered with precast concrete to increase strength to withstand earthquake loads, and to reduce seepage and therefore vulnerability to liquefaction. Two examples of BBB for irrigation canals in Nepal and Cambodia are provided in Box 3.

Box 3: Project Examples—Resilient Structures

The Asian Development Bank (ADB) 2009 **Nepal Emergency Flood Damage Rehabilitation Project** (43001-012) rehabilitated surface irrigation canals following severe floods that affected western Nepal. Flood-resistant design standards were adopted to rehabilitate farmland and the construction of infrastructure to reduce impacts from future flooding.

ADB's 2012 **Cambodia: Flood Damage Emergency Reconstruction Project** (46009-001) built back better by restoring livelihoods by increasing agriculture productivity and providing short-term income for the community who were employed in the construction of the canals, and by providing emergency access to communities in the event of future flooding. Upgrades in engineering design and stronger standards were paramount in restoring structures with climate-resilient features.

Sources: ADB. Nepal Emergency Flood Damage Rehabilitation Project; and ADB. Cambodia: Flood Damage Emergency Reconstruction Project.

Resilient Materials and Construction

Reconstruction and rehabilitation of irrigation systems, such as canal embankments and intake structures, allow for adoption of more resilient and durable materials to withstand future disasters (Box 4). One example is the replacement of brick with reinforced concrete and the use of geotextile membrane for canal foundations. It is essential to ensure however, that resilience of irrigation infrastructure is long-term and functional through construction that is of high quality and with materials and workmanship that have been properly tested and inspected. Monitoring by an independent third party is important for quality assurance (QA) purposes.

Box 4: Project Example—Resilient Materials and Construction

ADB Indonesia: Emergency Assistance for Rehabilitation and Reconstruction Project (52316-001).
The project supported the resilient reconstruction of the Gumbasa irrigation system in Central Sulawesi following the 2018 earthquake and tsunami.

In 2018, a 4.7 magnitude earthquake in Central Sulawesi Province, Indonesia, caused ruptures in the main and subsidiary crustal faults that run north to south, down the Palu valley. The area suffered from severe earth tremors that significantly damaged the Gumbasa irrigation system and the Palu, Sigi, and Donggala District (PASIGALA) area water supply system. Landslips, soil heaves, and the liquefaction of soil areas were believed to be saturated by percolation from the main canal.

The Asian Development Bank 2019 **Indonesia: Emergency Assistance for Rehabilitation and Reconstruction** project (52316-001) provided an evaluation of potential materials and construction methods to better withstand future earthquakes and liquefaction. Stone masonry structures of the Gumbasa irrigation system were restored and strengthened with reinforced concrete, and an impermeable membrane was applied to main and secondary canals to reduce percolation. High-risk areas of the PASIGALA pipeline crossing ground fault lines that traverse liquefaction areas were restructured with a high grade of polyethylene pipe (HDPE PE 100 PN 16 type), which is encased in sand and joins galvanized iron pipes to provide flexibility and full rotation.

Source: ADB. Indonesia: Emergency Assistance for Rehabilitation and Reconstruction.

ADB Viet Nam: Water Efficiency Improvement in Drought-Affected Provinces Project (49404-002).
Construction of cutting-edge, irrigation pressure pipelines aims to fortify drought resilience in Binh Thuan, a province severely impacted by drought.

Modernization

The opportunity to modernize agricultural systems can result in speedier, smarter, and more flexible responses to natural and climate change hazards, particularly with regard to irrigation system infrastructure and management. Improvement in areas such as water productivity and efficiency and the financial sustainability to cope with disaster impacts will, in turn, increase food production and financial returns to invest in the operation and maintenance of water supplies. This will help prevent the recurrence of the "build–neglect–rebuild" cycle where maintenance is not provided.

Key recommendations for surface irrigation systems include the installation of flow measurement devices and the adoption of real-time monitoring of canal and river flows to predict and respond to flood and drought occurrences more efficiently (Box 5). In upgrading control and safety systems, thought should be given to adding spillway and escape outlets of a higher capacity. Furthermore, the lining of canals and use of a pressure irrigation system to reduce distribution loss can be upgraded to address drought risk, in addition to use of pipes and/or enclosed canals to help conserve water by reducing water loss due to evaporation and seepage. Design improvements should be carried out in parallel to more efficient and effective information systems, including those relating to the forecasting of hazards and smart systems that are applied to monitor damage, thus facilitating repair and recovery efforts.

Box 5: Project Example—Irrigation Modernization

ADB Viet Nam: Water Efficiency Improvement in Drought-Affected Provinces Project (49404-002).
Construction of cutting-edge, irrigation pressure pipelines aims to fortify drought resilience in Binh Thuan,
a province severely impacted by drought.

The Southern Central Coast and Central Highlands of Viet Nam are particularly vulnerable to climate
change. The 2014–2016 El Niño Southern Oscillation (ENSO)-induced drought was the most severe
in 40 years, while rainfall during the 2015 monsoon period was 40%–70% below the long-term average.
Approximately 60,000 hectares of agricultural land in the central highlands was affected to varying
degrees. The impact was most severe on the smallholder farmers who rely on rain-fed surface water
sources for irrigation.

In response, the Asian Development Bank (ADB) 2018 **Viet Nam: Water Efficiency Improvement in
Drought-Affected Provinces Project** (49404-002) focused on sustainably improving the production of
water by modernizing irrigation infrastructure and strengthening irrigation management services, the latter
of which included the maintenance of irrigation systems, allocation of irrigation water, and water delivery
services. In addition, on-farm irrigation management practices have been upgraded.

The project aims to overhaul eight irrigation subprojects in five provinces to provide a higher level of
service (i.e., more flexible, reliable, and accessible supply of water) to farmers. Infrastructure works include
(i) pressurized pipe systems that connect canals or reservoirs with supply hydrants located in reasonable
proximity to farmers' fields; (ii) main system modernization, including canal lining, control structures,
storage, and installation of flow control and measurement devices with remote monitoring; and (iii) new
and more effective weirs to replace those constructed by farmers so that stored water can be pumped to
irrigate high-value crops.

Furthermore, the project will support policy and institutional development measures to improve
agriculture climate resilience, including allocation and delivery of water. This will be done by creating
a framework for irrigation water-sharing, as well as a support system in real time. System maintenance
will be improved by producing an inventory of and management database for assets, a structured
maintenance schedule for such assets, and a water pricing framework.

Source: ADB. Viet Nam: Water Efficiency Improvement in Drought-Affected Provinces Project.

Nature-Based Solutions

Nature-based solutions (NBS) mimic natural processes and build on land restoration and water-land operations management to improve vegetation, water availability and quality, and raise agricultural productivity. In relation to irrigated agriculture, NBS can increase the availability of water through, for example, soil moisture retention, groundwater recharge, small storage structures, and rainwater harvesting (Box 6). They also can improve water quality in natural and constructed wetlands and riparian buffer strips, as well as reduce the risks associated with water-related disasters and climate change (e.g., floodplain restoration, green roofs and canal bank protection with deep rooting grasses, trees, and hydrophytes).[13] In disaster recovery terms, NBS may complement engineering measures for resilience and improve longer-term watershed and irrigation system sustainability (e.g., restoration of inactive floodplains enhancing retention and improving water quality)

Box 6: Project Example—Nature-Based Solutions

The Kyrgyz Republic, particularly the southern *oblasts* (provinces) of Jalal-Abad and Osh, is highly prone to landslides because of its rainfall patterns, geology, land cover, and high seismic activity. There are more than 4,500 landslide sites in the country, of which about 1,200 are active. Approximately 550 settlements, housing 30,000 people and representing approximately 30% of settlements and 0.5% of total population, face immediate landslide risk.

The Asian Development Bank **Kyrgyz Republic: Landslide Risk Management Sector Project** (53022-001) aims to reduce exposure of at-risk communities (involving 15–20 subprojects) to landslides through mitigation engineering measures. Where appropriate, nature-based solutions, such as regreening and timber retaining and drainage structures, will be carried out.

Source: ADB. Kyrgyz Republic: Landslide Risk Management Sector Project.

Early Warning Systems

Early warning systems (EWS) using integrated communication systems to help communities and institutions to prepare for hazardous climate-related events are an important part of building resilient agricultural and irrigation systems and disaster risk management. Their key elements include risk knowledge, monitoring and data acquisition, forecasting and warning methods, dissemination and communication processes, information, and response capacity. Early warning systems often utilize cutting edge technology for hazard modeling; monitoring and observation by using remote sensing and ground stations (aided by geographic information systems); and digital transformation, including cloud computing.[14]

---

[13] United Nations Educational, Scientific and Cultural Organization. 2018. Nature-Based Solutions for Water. In *The United Nations World Water Development Report 2018*.

[14] ADB. 2020. *Mongolia: Strengthening Integrated Early Warning System in Mongolia* (53039-002).

For irrigated agriculture, EWS include warning systems for geophysical and extreme weather events as well as seasonal monitoring for droughts. For example, the South Asia Drought Monitoring System, launched by the International Water Management Institute, provides a weekly map of drought conditions in the region. It also includes advanced global drought monitoring and decision-making tools in the form of indexes such as the Integrated Drought Severity Index, Standardized Precipitation Index, and Soil Moisture Index.[15] Such tools can be integrated into post-disaster recovery processes to improve future forecasting and preparedness.

Communication and dissemination of risk information is a critical element of EWS operation. Roles and responsibilities should be clear for media, government institutions, water users, etc., and telecommunication networks should be sufficiently capable to reach farming communities. Capacity building of water users and system operators is important to ensure that they have the necessary knowledge to respond to early warnings, such as modifications to the dates for planting and harvesting and the areas to be cropped in response to prolonged drought conditions. An example of EWS BBB support in Bangladesh that incorporated capacity building is provided in Box 7.

Box 7: Project Example—Early Warning and Monitoring Systems

The Asian Development Bank 2005 **Bangladesh: Emergency Flood Damage Rehabilitation Project** (38625-013) provided analytical input and capacity building to enhance existing early warning systems, including the flood forecasting system operated by the Flood Forecasting and Warning Centre under the Bangladesh Water Development Board.

The project included improving reliability of the existing forecasting system, improving accuracy of weather predictions, and providing longer forecasting periods. It also determined cost-effective options to update the 40-year-old topographic and elevation data, and linked the existing flood forecasting system to major infrastructure and agricultural land to improve its usefulness.

Source: ADB. Bangladesh: Emergency Flood Damage Rehabilitation Project.

Strengthening Resilient Management

Strengthening irrigation system management is essential to strengthen resilience to natural hazards, as well as to improve productivity and sustainability. Large-scale surface irrigation systems are typically developed and managed by government institutions, such as the irrigation ministry or equivalent, with farmers responsible for their own on-farm irrigation. While the formation of water user groups has been widely promoted in recent decades as a shift away from lower-level system management roles, it has met varying degrees of success. Often, systems are constrained by the lack of capacity and underinvestment in repairs and maintenance, thus increasing vulnerability to extreme events, such as floods and drought.

---

[15]   International Water Management Institute. Digital Data and Tools. http:// www.iwmi.cgiar.org/resources/data-and-tools (accessed July 2021).

Strengthening management at the system and farm levels will ensure improved resilience, continuity of water service delivery, and adequacy of repairs and maintenance through prioritization of planning and use of water resources, and management of irrigation and other facilities. It often involves refining system monitoring and scheduling by developing processes for real-time irrigation scheduling and the use of prepaid water usage metering. Capacity building for government institutions, farmer stakeholders, and water user groups is central to achieving improved system management. An example of such an approach delivered in Viet Nam is provided in Box 8.

Box 8: Project Example—Strengthening Resilient Management

ADB Viet Nam: Water Efficiency Improvement in Drought-Affected Provinces Project (49404-002). Construction of cutting-edge, irrigation pressure pipelines aims to fortify drought resilience in Binh Thuan, a province severely impacted by drought.

The Asian Development Bank 2018 **Viet Nam: Water Efficiency Improvement in Drought-Affected Provinces Project** (49404-002) exemplifies the complementarity between the modernization of irrigation systems and their management in order to build resilience.

The project aims to strengthen management practices by improving water allocation and delivery services by way of a real-time decision support system for farmers, so that they are able to optimize crop water applications. Maintenance of systems will be upgraded by applying asset inventory and management databases, as well as a systematic asset maintenance schedule and funding approach that is based on asset condition assessments. A water pricing framework and options to engage third parties in the operation and maintenance areas also will be established.

Source: ADB. Viet Nam: Water Efficiency Improvement in Drought-Affected Provinces Project.

Risk-Informed Governance

Post-disaster recovery efforts can support and strengthen disaster risk governance for irrigated agricultural systems by developing preparedness plans, protocols for irrigation system operation, and essential procedures for emergency events. This requires development of a comprehensive multihazard risk assessment; asset inventories, including identifying key assets vulnerable to hazards; disaster response strategies; institutional roles and responsibilities; and an effective communication approach (e.g., use of mobile and web-based networks to disseminate information to system operators and water users). These should be supported by comprehensive capacity building of system management and water users. Box 9 provides a comprehensive case study of BBB for irrigation systems in Cambodia, which incorporated considerations around governance and capacity.

Box 9: Case Study—Comprehensive Build Back Better for Irrigation Systems

The floods of 2011 in Cambodia caused severe damage to rural infrastructure, amounting to $376 million, and affecting more than 1.7 million people in 18 of Cambodia's 24 provinces. There was extensive suffering among the local population, with serious interruption of key economic activities. From late September to mid-October 2013, further serious flash floods occurred, caused by heavy rainfall combined with runoff from neighboring Thailand into Cambodia's northwestern provinces. These floods were more sudden and intense than the 2011 floods. The result was that 20 of the country's 24 provinces were impacted, with total damage and loss to public infrastructure estimated at $356 million.

In an effort to rapidly and effectively restore economic activities following the 2011 flooding, the Asian Development Bank (ADB) launched the **Cambodia: Flood Damage Emergency Reconstruction Project**[a] (46009-001 and 46009-003) in March 2012, with financing[b] in the amount of $72 million. In 2013 at the government's request and based on project performance, ADB approved an additional financing[c] in the amount of $83 million. Output 3 of the project focused on restoration and improvement of a select number of irrigation schemes and provision of better flood management against existing hydrological and meteorological (hydromet) hazards.[d] It had been found that the factors contributing to irrigation scheme damage were the inadequate spillways to cope with peak discharges, incorrect operation of head regulators, insufficient escapes for discharge of flow surcharges, rapid flow divergence leading to erosion of structures, and highly erodible unlined canals.

The project aimed to build back better in a manner that will protect against future flooding. Engineering designs addressed not only the restoration of infrastructure to pre-flood conditions but also, in many cases, design upgrades while incorporating the means for low maintenance. Overall scheme resilience was strengthened through capacity building of water user communities and improving early warning systems.

Restoration of damaged infrastructure was divided into three stages. Stage 1 involved the immediate repair of infrastructure on a temporary basis and restoration of communications. Stage 2 involved the fast-tracking of repairs to restore functionality before the start of the next wet season so as to secure existing works. Stage 3 involved the completion of flood damage restoration over the next two dry seasons. Flood capacity of key structures was upgraded and improved, and operation plans and discharge capacity were reviewed.

continued on next page

Box 9 *continued*

Photo 1: Ang Trapaing Thmor Dam. Reservoir embankment prior to repair.

Photo 1: Ang Trapaing Thmor Dam. Reservoir embankment after repair.

By project completion, 35 flood-damaged schemes had been rehabilitated and 69,157 hectares (ha) irrigated. This is equivalent to 111% of the targeted area (62,500 ha)—of which 43,560 ha and 25,597 ha related to wet and dry season cropping, respectively. In terms of farmer water user communities, 21 were strengthened and provided with seven new water user buildings. A total of 4,116 farmers, including 1,713 (42%) women farmers, were trained to operate and maintain the rehabilitated irrigation schemes. Hydomet system improvements included installation of 10 stations and 8 automatic weather stations to provide real-time feedback of rainfall and river flow data; more accurate peak flow frequency estimates; and early warnings of future flood events. They fall under the responsibility of the Department of Hydrology and River Works (Ministry of Water Resources and Meteorology).

One of the rehabilitated schemes (Ang Trapaing Thmor, a natural reservoir) not only supports agricultural activities but also provides flood protection of National Road N5 between Siem Reap and Banteay Meanchey provinces, as well as neighboring rice fields and villages. The scheme's dam embankment was extensively damaged by floods in 2013 due to the malfunction of sluice gates; water levels rose to less than 0.5 meters freeboard, resulting in wave damage over much of the embankment. Forced and uncontrolled opening of gates also resulted in release of flood waves, leading to inundation of main canals and damage to embankments, flow control, and drainage structures.

Stage 2 project activities gave priority to restoration of the dam embankment, whereby a cut-off trench for seepage control (3,500 meters) was installed, as were a gabion mattress and boxes for wave protection; and the dam crest level (3,000 meters) was restored (Photo 1 and Photo 2). Stage 3, based on updated hydrologic design criteria, included further extension of the embankment cut-off drains and gabion protection, repair and improvement of sluice gates, and repair of the main canal and four of the drain embankments and structures.

The quality of rehabilitated irrigation infrastructure was deemed acceptable by beneficiaries and local authorities alike who, together with various consultants, took part in the design, supervision, and quality control of the scheme. It is estimated that a total of 93,740 farmers benefitted directly from these efforts, of whom more than 50% were women.

continued on next page

Box 9 *continued*

Lessons Learned from the Project

- The combined expertise of engineers and other specialists, together with local knowledge, substantially benefitted the design of a subproject.
- In the absence of hydrological data for designs and studies to mitigate risk in emergency rehabilitation projects, projects should exclude (or consider less of a priority) those subproject areas that often have been deeply inundated over the previous 10 years.
- In flood-prone areas, climate-resilient infrastructure should be built according to design and material standards and specifications that can adapt to increased runoff or water flow during flood periods.
- Engineering designs should consider the capacity of government in allocating maintenance budgets.
- The network of hydromet and automatic weather stations is essential for the future design and development of irrigation and road networks. Statistical analyses to determine return periods and monitor climate change should take into account historical data—at least 10 to 20 years.
- Irrigation systems depend on efficient and effective operation and maintenance, manuals for which are vital to ensure correct operation, particularly as regards flood gates and their management.

[a] ADB. Cambodia: Flood Damage Emergency Reconstruction Project.
[b] ADB's special fund resource of $67.20 million, in addition to a grant of $5.25 million from the Government of Australia.
[c] ADB's special fund resource of $75 million, in addition to a grant of $6.68 million from the Government of Australia.
[d] Output 1 and output 2 relate to national roads and rural road reconstruction, respectively.

Source: Asian Development Bank.

SUGGESTED READINGS

The following technical and subject matter resources are further references in implementing nonstructural build back better measures.

Asian Development Bank (ADB). 2011. Water Operational Plan 2011–2020.

ADB. 2015. *Innovations for More Food with Less Water Project: Task 2 Synthesis Report.*

ADB. 2015. Nepal: Innovations for More Food with Less Water—Task 2 Final Report.

ADB. 2018. Strategy 2030: Achieving a Prosperous, Inclusive, Resilient, and Sustainable Asia and the Pacific.

ADB. 2020. Technical Assistance to Mongolia for Strengthening Integrated Early Warning System in Mongolia.

C. Burt. 2001. Rapid Appraisal Process (RAP) and Benchmarking: Explanation and Tools. *ITRC Report.* No. R 01-008. Irrigation Training and Research Center, California Polytechnic State University.

Food and Agriculture Organization of the United Nations (FAO). 2018. Nature-Based Solutions for Agricultural Water Management and Food Security. *Land and Water Discussion Paper.* Series 12.

FAO. 2021. Nature-Based Solutions in Agriculture: Sustainable Management and Conservation of Land, Water, and Biodiversity.

Global Facility for Disaster Reduction and Recovery. 2018. Building Back Better in Post-Disaster Recovery: Achieving Resilience through Stronger, Faster, and More Inclusive Post-Disaster Reconstruction.

International Water Management Institute. Digital Data and Tools.

Mott MacDonald. 2017. *Framework for Effectiveness and Resilience of Small and Medium Irrigation in Nepal: RSAS 0017 Final Report.*

C. Popovska, M. Jovanovski, and D. Sekovski. 2019. Build Back Better Approach to Recovery of Flood-Damaged Transport and Water Infrastructure. Paper presented at the Water Management and Hydraulic Engineering Conference.

UNEP-DHI Centre. 2013. *Climate-Resilient Irrigation Guidance Paper—Final*. Coastal Adaptation and Resilience Planning Component.

United Nations Educational, Scientific and Cultural Organization. 2018. Nature-Based Solutions for Water. In *The United Nations World Water Development Report 2018*.